LIZARD INVASION

By Marta Magellan
Illustrated by Mauro Magellan

Eifrig Publishing LLC
Lemont

At Eifrig Publishing, our motto is our mission —
"Good for our kids, good for our Earth, and good for our communities."
We are passionate about helping kids develop into caring, creative, thoughtful individuals who possess positive self-images, celebrate differences, and practice inclusion. Our books promote social and environmental consciousness and empower children as they grow in their communities.
www.eifrigpublishing.com

© 2025 New Edition, Marta Magellan
Printed in the United States of America

All rights reserved. This publication is protected by Copyright, and permission should be obtained from the publisher prior to any prohibited reproduction, storage in a retrieval system, or transmission in any form or by any means, electronic, mechanical, photocopying, recording, or likewise.

Published by Eifrig Publishing,
PO Box 66, Lemont, PA 16851, USA

For information regarding permission, write to:
Rights and Permissions Department,
Eifrig Publishing,
PO Box 66, Lemont, PA 16851, USA.
permissions@eifrigpublishing.com

Library of Congress Cataloging-in-Publication Data
Magellan, Marta
Lizard Invasion: Florida's Little Green Anoles and Their Fight for Survival
by Marta Magellan, illustrated by Mauro Magellan
p. cm.

978-1-63233-406-0   Paperback $12.99
978-1-63233-407-7   Hardcover $18.99
978-1-63233-408-4   ebook $2.99

Originally published as *Anole Invasion*, 2018:
ISBN 978-1-63233-187-8

[1. Nature - Juvenile Nonfiction. 2. Animals - Anoles, Lizards, Pollinators - Juvenile Nonfiction
I. Magellan, Mauro, ill. II. Title

29 28 27 26 2025
5 4 3 2 1

Printed on recycled PCW acid-free paper. ∞

To Sammy Joe Schnall —Nana
To Tracy Joy —Mauro

Anole: A small lizard that lives in bushes and climbs trees.

Professionals who study these lizards say:
"ah-NOLE" as in "a pole."

You might hear others pronounce the name this way:
"ah-No-lee" as in "guacamole."

A Green Anole watches a cricket crawl on a branch. The cricket doesn't know it's in danger.

Wild lizards don't have names, but let's call this Green Anole 'Carolina', because it is sometimes known by its common name, Carolina Anole.

She stays so still that the cricket doesn't know she's there. Without a sound, she attacks.

The cricket is a goner.

Green Anoles like Carolina love crickets and beetles and moths. They even eat cockroaches and do not throw up!

Anoles also go from flower to flower sipping sweet **nectar**. When they do, they act as unintentional **pollinators**. That means they spread **pollen**, the often yellow powder needed to make seeds.

Green Anoles are good for plants, but it's about to become harder for Carolina and her friends to visit their usual flowers.

Carolina watches as a small brown lizard scurries through the brush in her **territory** (the area where she lives). The **male** Brown Anole bobs his head up and down, does a few push-ups, and flashes his orange **dewlap** (throat fan).

It is a warning.

Carolina turns from green to gray to tan, and finally to dark brown. The invading lizard has put her in a very bad mood!

Green Anole turned brown

Chameleon

Green Anoles change colors when they feel threatened or sick, or too hot. Because of that, some people call Green Anoles 'chameleons'. But they are not true chameleons. True chameleons can turn many different colors.

So who was this brown lizard that didn't turn colors at all?

The stranger is a Cuban Brown Anole. It is taking Carolina's territory! Over time, Carolina sees more strange lizards like him. Those Brown Anoles weren't in the United States at first.

It is called an **invasion**. How did that happen?

Brown Anole

About a hundred years ago in Cuba, a Brown Anole hitched a ride on a boat. Let's call her Cubanita.

As Cubanita set out, the ocean stretched out all around her. Soon, the boat docked. Cubanita quickly sped off the boat and looked around her new home. Where was she?

The place was warm, humid, and full of palm trees and shrubs. She had landed in Florida. She found some moist leaf litter and laid an egg.

Every week or two during that summer, she laid one or two eggs. Over time, little Brown Anoles were everywhere. Then, a bigger, more agressive anole invaded Florida.

In the 1950's, the big-headed Knight Anole hitched a ride to Florida, too. It also came from Cuba. It became more of a threat because it eats the smaller anoles!

But that's not all. It eats frogs and baby birds, too.

That wasn't the last of the invasions.

Around 1975, a new enemy invaded, this time from Puerto Rico. The Crested Anole fought harder and ran faster than both the Green and Brown Anoles.

After the Puerto Rican Crested Anoles invaded, Brown Anoles moved to middle levels of the plants and trees. Other anoles have also entered Florida, like the Bark Anole from Haiti and the Giant Anole from Jamaica. Even more will likely continue to move into the state.

There isn't enough food in the lower plants for all of them to share. Carolina and her relatives had to find another way to stay alive.

Puerto Rican Crested Anole

Invaders are not good for native Green Anoles like Carolina. The different **species** (types) of lizards compete for the same food. Worse, the non-native anoles eat the eggs of the Green Anole. Other invaders, like the Curly-Tailed Lizard and the Peter's Rock Agama are also in Florida posing a threat. They both eat smaller anoles. The invaders eat more of the food. So the Green Anoles have to climb higher up in the plants, and even higher in the trees.

This is called **displacement.** And that's trouble.

Cuban Brown Anoles have now spread out to other parts of the southern United States. Crested Anoles and Knight Anoles have wandered north to Central Florida. They are roaming even farther up, displacing more Green Anoles.

When invasive species have been living in a place long enough, scientists say they are **established**.

To stay alive among so many invaders, Green Anoles did some amazing things.

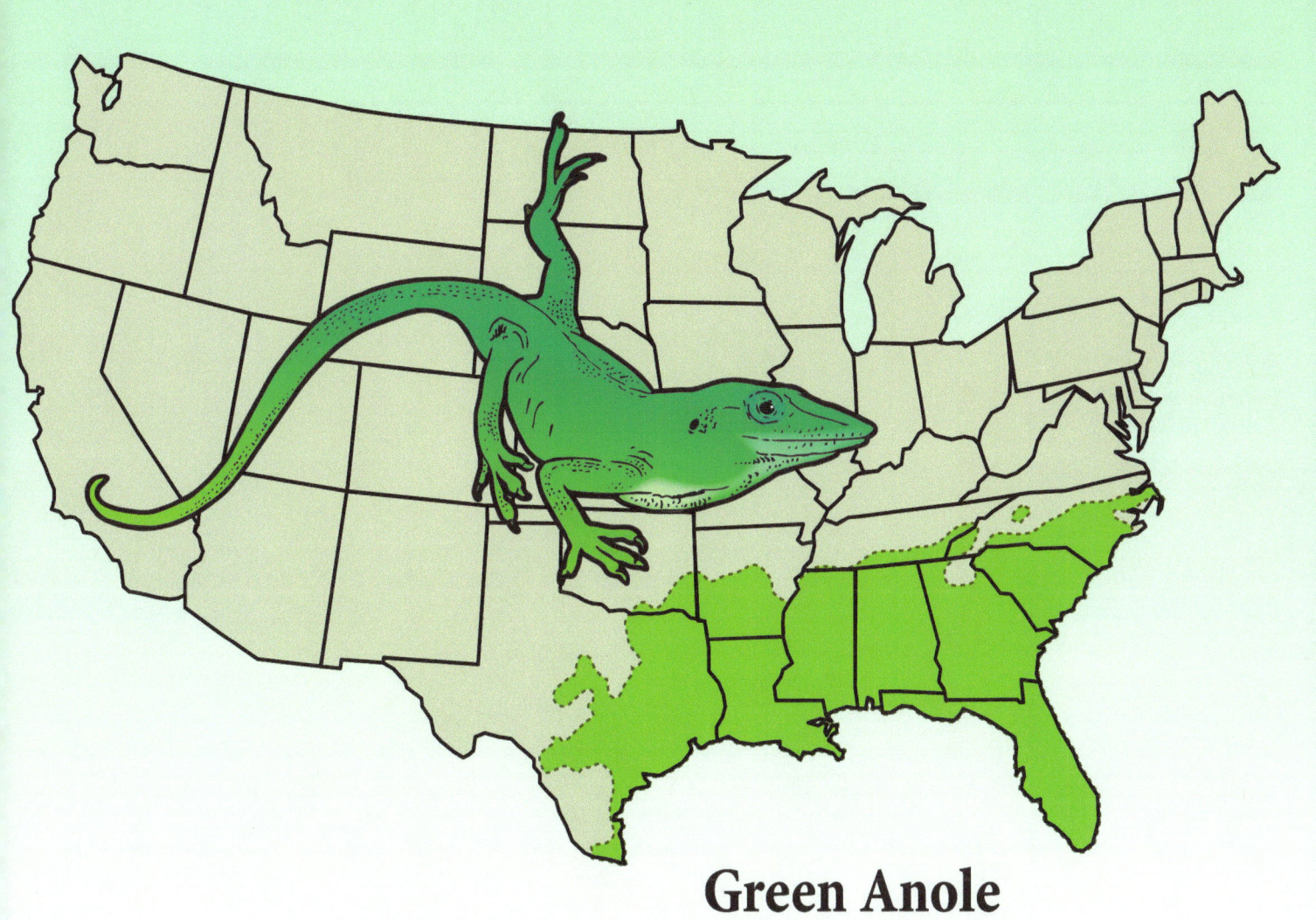

Green Anole
Anolis carolinensis

They **adapted** to their new situation by climbing higher up in trees where there was more food and less competition. They even **evolved** sticky feet to hang on the trunks easier. In South Florida, the Green and Brown Anoles have even mixed together. Those are called **hybrids**.

Green Anoles did whatever they could to survive.

But their troubles are not over. More and bigger lizards keep showing up in Green Anole territory. Florida has more non-native species of reptiles living in the wild than anywhere else in the world. One reason for that is that people like having reptiles for pets. When pets like the Green Iguana and the Burmese Python escape or are let loose, they cause harm to the native species. People must be careful not to let non-native species overrun native territories.

The good news is Green Anoles are not **endangered.** Not yet. As long as they continue adapting and evolving, we will continue to see them in our gardens, helping plants grow.

Six Non-native Lizards in Florida

Peter's Rock Agama: *Agama picticauda*

A medium-sized lizard, breeding males have an orange head, a blue body, and a tri-colored tail. It was introduced from Africa for the pet trade due to the male's colorful appearance. After escaping or being let loose, they are now spreading rapidly throughout Florida. They eat many types of insects as well as smaller lizards like the Brown Anole.

Knight Anole: *Anolis equestris equestris*

The largest of all anoles, it measures as much as twenty inches long. It turns from bright green to brown depending on mood, stress level, and temperature. Originally from Cuba, it has become an invasive species in several Florida counties and has also spread to some southeastern states. It not only eats the same food as Green Anoles, but it eats Green Anoles, too. It also preys on frogs and baby birds.

Brown Basilisk: *Basiliscus vittatus*

This brown or striped lizard with a crest on its head has large hind feet with flaps of skin on the toes. It is famous for appearing to walk on water. Because of this, it is often called the Jesus Christ Lizard. Studies show this species may carry disease, like the West Nile virus. Brought in for the pet trade, it has been able to live and breed successfully in Florida.

Northern Curly-Tailed Lizard: *Leiocephalus carinatus*

Native to the Caribbean, this small, mottled brown-gray lizard is named for its tail that curls upward. It was introduced to Palm Beach, Florida in the early 1940s to combat sugar cane pests. It then spread south. It feeds on insects and other small lizards.

Green Iguana: *Iguana iguana*

This is a very large green or orange lizard native to Central and South America. Due to its notable dinosaur-like appearance, it was brought to the United States for the pet trade. Often released into the wild when they got too big for their owners, the Green Iguana is now established in South Florida. It can grow as much as seven feet long and weigh up to twenty pounds. Their burrows destroy sidewalks, seawalls, and foundations.

Puerto Rican Crested Anole: *Anolis cristatellus*

A small, brownish lizard originally from Puerto Rico, it is now established in Florida and competes with the Brown Anole. The male often has a crest running down the top of the tail, which is how it got its name. Like the Brown Anole, it probably entered the state unintentionally on imported landscape plants and cargo ships.

Glossary

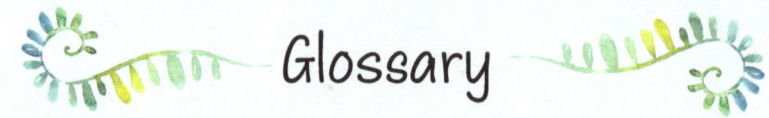

Adapt/Adapted: When living things change over time to live in new situations or territories. Green Anoles adapted when they moved higher up in the trees.

Dewlap: A usually bright colored flap of skin on the throat that lizards display on purpose to communicate. It flares out like a fan when the male lizard feels threatened or wants to attract a mate.

Displacement: When two competing species want to live in the same place, the weaker animal will be forced to move to new territory, because there are not enough places to live or food to share.

Endangered: A plant or animal species in danger of becoming extinct.

Evolve/Evolved: When living things change over a long time to help them survive. Green Anoles grew sticky feet over time to help them hang out in trees.

Extinct: When the last member of a species has died and that animal no longer exists.

Female: The sex of an animal, which produces eggs.

Habitat: The place where animals, plants, and living things make their home.

Hybrid: Something that is made by mixing two different things. Living things can merge to become hybrids, such as the Green and Brown Anoles.

Invasive/Invasion: When non-native species have been brought to a location by humans and become so successful that they displace the native species.

Male: The sex of an animal that fertilizes the female's eggs, which turns them into neonates (offspring).

Native: In biology, it means animals that normally have lived in a particular location for hundreds of years or more and were not brought in by humans.

Non-native: Species of animals and plants living outside their native homes. Not all non-natives become invasive, but those that do can harm our gardens and natural areas.

Pollen: a powder made by flowers to help plants make seeds and grow new plants. Although most commonly yellow, pollen comes in many colors.

Pollinator: An animal like a bee or a hummingbird, or even an anole, that helps plants make seeds, which makes more plants.

Species: A group of closely related animals that are physically similar and are capable of reproducing (having offspring).

Territory: An area where a single animal or group of the same species lives and defends against invaders.

ABOUT THE AUTHOR AND ILLUSTRATOR

Author Marta Magellan and Illustrator Mauro Magellan are a brother and sister team who have collaborated on award-winning picture books focused on conservation and wildlife. They also write separately. Marta now writes full time after spending most of her career teaching English Composition and Creative Writing at Miami Dade College. Mauro is a songwriter as well as an author and illustrator. He's also a musician and has played drums with bands such as the *Georgia Satellites* and *Dan Baird and Homemade Sin*.

ABOUT THE SCIENCE EDITOR

Kirsten Hines is an award-winning author, wildlife photographer, and conservationist with an M.Sc. in biology and background in environmental education. Her writing and photography have appeared in numerous publications, including her eight books on Florida's nature and history such as *Birds of Florida*, *Wild Florida: An Animal Odyssey*, and *Attracting Birds to South Florida Gardens*. She aims to inspire conservation action through her storytelling, wildlife-oriented presentations, trips and workshops, and not-for-profit work.

ABOUT THE DESIGNER

Tamian Wood uses art, photography, typography, and digital collage techniques to create books that sell, in a wide variety of genres. With over 30 years in the design trenches, she is an active member of the Editorial Freelancers Association (EFA) and a proud member of Phi Theta Kappa National Honour Society. She holds degrees in Computer Science and Graphic Design Technology,

SELECTED REFERENCES

Bock, Dan, et. al. (2021) "Changes in selection pressure can facilitate hybridization during biological invasion in a Cuban lizard." *Proceedings of the National Academy of Sciences.* https://doi.org/10.1073/pnas.2108638118

Kearney, Bill. (2024) "The lizard wars of South Florida help reveal how evolution works." *South Florida Sun Sentinel.* https://www.sun-sentinel.com/2024/11/30/the-lizard-wars

Learn Rapp, J. (2021, Mar.) "Densely Packed Invasive Anoles Outcompete Natives." *The Wildlife Society.* https://wildlife.org.denseley-packed-anoles-outcompete-natives/

Mazzotti, Frank and Harvey, R. (2024, Nov.) "The Invasion of Exotic Reptiles and Amphibians in Florida." *AskIFAS.* University of Florida. https://doi.org/10.32473/edis-uw365-2012

Stroud, James et al, (2024). "Observing character displacement from process to pattern in a novel vertebrate community." *Nature Communications.* doi.org/10.1038/s41467-024-54302-1

*Websites active at time of publication

ACKNOWLEDGMENTS

Thank you to the librarians at the St. John's County Library System and the St. Augustine Garden Club for being instrumental in bringing this book into the hands of children. Special thanks to Cathy Snyder, whose hospitality and passion for imparting knowledge through the Nature Detectives workshops, has been a constant inspiration for me. I am also grateful to scientist and wildlife photographer, Kirsten Hines, who not only edited the information for accuracy, but also provided some beautiful photographs. Also, thankful to my husband whose photographs adorn this and many of my books. As always, my profound gratitude to Penny Eifrig, whose belief in doing well by children and conserving our planet has made this book possible. No acknowledgment could be complete without mention of my children and grandchildren. It is for them and future generations that I became interested in writing books that focus on protecting the biodiversity of our planet.

Watercolor Leaf Assets by Octopus Artis via designcuts.com

Index

(numbers in bold refer to photographs or illustrations)

adaptation, adapting, 24, 25
Bark Anole, 18
Brown Anole, Cuban brown anole, 8, **9**, 12, **13**, 14, 18, 22
chameleon, **10**, 11
color change, 11
competetion, compete, 21, 22, 24
Cuba, 14, 17
dewlap, 8, **13**
displacement, 21
eggs, 14, 15, 21
endangered, 25
established, 22
Florida, 14, 17, 18, 21, 22, 25, 28
flowers, plants, 6, 7, 14, 18, 21, 25
food, **4**, 5, 6, **7**, 17, 18, 21
Giant Anole, 18
Green Anole, Carolina Anole, 5, 6, **7**, 8, **9,** 18, **20**, 21, 22, **23**, 24, 25
invasion, invaders, 12, 14, 17, 18, 21, 22
Knight Anole, **16**, 17, 22
male, 8
nectar, 6
pollen, pollinators, 6, **7**
Puerto Rico, 18
Puerto Rican Crested Anole, 18, **19**
species, 21, 24
territory, 8, 12, 18, 21, 22, **23**, 25

www.ingramcontent.com/pod-product-compliance
Lightning Source LLC
Chambersburg PA
CBHW041602070526
44586CB00003BA/55